*

THREAD THAT BINDS

By

J.J.BHATT

ISBN:

9798393129187

Title:

Thread That Binds

Author:

J.J. Bhatt

Published and Distributed by Amazon and Kindle worldwide.

This book is manufactured in the Unites States of America.

Recent Books by J.J. Bhatt

HUMAN ENDEAVOR: *Essence & Mission/ A Call for Global Awakening, (*2011)

ROLLING SPIRITS: *Being Becoming* /A Trilogy, (2012)

ODYSSEY OF THE DAMNED: *A Revolving Destiny,* (2013).

PARISHRAM: *Journey of the Human Spirits*, (2014).

TRIUMPH OF THE BOLD: *A Poetic Reality*, (2015).

THEATER OF WISDOM, *(2016).*

MAGNIFICENT QUEST: *Life, Death & Eternity,* (2016).

ESSENCE OF INDIA: *A Comprehensive Perspective,* (2016).

ESSENCE OF CHINA: *Challenges & Possibilities*, (2016).

BEING & MORAL PERSUASION: *A Bolt of Inspiration*, (2017).

REFELCTIONS, RECOLLECTIONS & EXPRESSIONS, (2018).

ONE, TWO, THREE... ETERNITY: *A Poetic Odyssey, (*2018).

INDIA: *Journey of Enlightenment*, (2019a).

SPINNING MIND, SPINNING TIME: *C'est la vie*, (2019b).Book 1.

MEDITATION ON HOLY TRINITY, *(2019c), Book 2.*

ENLIGHTENMENT: *Fiat lux*, (2019d), Book 3.

BEING IN THE CONTEXTUAL ORBIT: *Rhythm, Melody & Meaning, (*2019e).

QUINTESSENCE: *Thought & Action,* (2019f).

THE WILL TO ASCENT: *Power of Boldness & Genius,* (2019g).

RIDE ON A SPINNING WHEEL: *Existence Introspected, (*2020a).

A FLASH OF LIGHT: *Splendors, Perplexities & Riddles,* (2020b).

ON A ZIG ZAG TRAIL: *The Flow of Life,* (2020c).

UNBOUNDED: *An Inner Sense of Destiny* (2020d).

REVERBERATIONS: The *Cosmic Pulse,* (2020e).

LIGHT & DARK: *Dialogue and Meaning,* (2021a).

ROLLING REALITY: *Being in flux, (2021b).*

FORMAL SPLENDOR: *The Inner Rigor,* (2021c).

TEMPORAL TO ETERNAL: *Unknown Expedition,* (2021d).

TRAILBLAZERS: *Spears of Courage,* (2021e).

TRIALS & ERRORS: *A Path to Human Understanding,* (2021f).

MEASURE OF HUMAN EXPERIENCE: *Brief Notes,* (2021g).

LIFE: *An Ellipsis (2022a).*

VALIDATION: *The Inner Realm of Essence* (2022b).

LET'S ROLL: *Brave Heart,* (2022c).

BEING BECOMING, (2022d).

INVINCIBLE, (2022e)/ THE CODE: *DESTINY,* (2022f).

LIFE DIMYSTIFIED, (2022g) / ESSENTIAL HUMANITY, (2022h).

MORAL ADVENTURE, (2022i / SPIRALING SPHERES (2022h).

EPHEMERAL SPLENDOR, (2023a / *CHAOTIC HARMONY*, (2023b).
Intellectual Mysticism (2023c) / *Will to Believe* (2023d)
Expectations & Reality (2023e) / **Thread** *That Binds* (2023f).

PREFACE

THREAD THAT BINDS explores significance of humanity as such in terms of its power of moral will and endless possibilities; permitting to grasp, "What is it all about?" Moreover it must be understood the stated thread is not fragile, but the very giant leap of our reality; an unifying force.

Apodictically speaking, the stated thin thread that binds is the source of, "Awakening, albeit what is our Truth." In this context, let the young minds be inspired to introspect their own meaning of existence; justifying the conquest of their respective mind for the greater good of the whole. Let them seize the moment, and stay on their set common destiny until the noble mission is successfully attended.

J.J. Bhatt

CONTENTS

Preface 5
Miracle Gift........... 11
Journey Beyond 12
Force that Binds....... 13
Introspection 14
Reflection 15
Reciprocity............ 16
The Blueprint 17
Renaissance 18
Love, Eternal 19
Missing Variable..... 20
Noble Path 21
Serendipity 22
Covenant............. 23
Infinity 24
Irony of Fate......... 25
Fulfillment 26
Blind Alley 27
Touch-stone 28
Discovery 29
The Drama 30
Being & Spirit....... 31
Big Question 32
Ruminations 33
Our Journey........ 34
Being in............ 35
Law of Life........ 36
Contemplation.... .. 37
Monkey Mind......... 38
Keep Marching....... 39
Forever............... 40
Pensive 41
Fragmented 42
Great Passage 43
Life is funny .... .44
Time to Spark......... 45
Morning Stroll 46
Be Human 47
The Spirit .... .48
What's the point? ... 49
Fortitude 50
Loves Destiny.......... 51
Our Reality 52
Only for you......... . 53
Fearless Bird 54
Nothing so New ... 55
Our Time 56
Dear Lady 57
Welcome 58
Ascension 59
Splendor of............ 60
Being & Meaning...... 61
The Bliss 62
Decoded 63
Sakshi 64
Admonition 65

Miracle 66
Liberation............... .67
Walk the Walk.......... 68
Bold Necessity.......... 69
Great Ride 70
The Flow................ 71
Being & Truth.......... 72
Affirmation............. 73
Everyman's Song...... 74
Dancers 75
The Curse............... 76
Sometimes 77
Force to be.............. 78
Timeless................. .79
Stand Tall............... 80
Glow in Dark .... .81
Essence.................. 82
Turbulence to........... 83
Pre-requisites......... 84
Beware.................. 85
Revival 86
Anniversary 87
The Gist............ ... 88
The Mirror 89
New Journey 90
To be.................. 91
Facilitator............... 92
That's Love.............. 93
Still on the Trail 94
Be Inspired 95
The Quest 96
Peel off Illusion......... 97
Fearless.................... 98
Unsettled 99
Spontaneity 100
The Code .... .101
Take Note 102
Moral Reference........ 103
Paradise 104
The Grasp 105
Each Step................ 106
Sinners & 107
Synergy 108
Back Off 109
Best Lovers............ 110
A View 111
Beware 112
Off the Cage.......... 113
Half-way............... 114
Open-up 115
Ramifications ...... .116
Twists & Turns...... . 117

Being & Perfection ……….. 118
Conditional Journey……….. 119
Let Go ……………………. 120
Voyagers………………… 121
Jewel …………………….. 122
Sentient ……………... 123
Quintessence …………... 124
Some Issues ……………… 125
Missing Variable………… 126
Will to Believe ………….. 127
End Game ………………. 128
No Escape……………….. 129
The Thread……………….. 130
Direction ………………… 131
Awakening ……………… 132
Thrust Foreword ………… 133
Be Confident ……………. 134
Adaptability …………… 135
Fortitude ………………… 136
Renewal ……………….. 137
Magic, it is…………….. 138
The Vibes………………. 139
Big Leap ………………. 140
Excelsior ………………. 141
"I," What it is………….. 142
Finite to Infinite………... 143
Moral Will …………… 144
The Awakened ………… 145
Noble Worth …………….146
Resilience …………… 147
Invention …………..148
Steep-climb ……... ..149
Juggernaut ……….. 150
Subjective Being… ..151
The Stigma ……….. 152
Conquer the ……… 153
Destiny …………… 154
Background……..... 155

Miracle Gift

Being,
What a miracle
Gift in the universe
Albeit, he's the
Ultimate moral agent
To turn expectations
Into reality

Being,
What a magic
Born to discover,
"The Self and the
Million unknowns"

Being,
What an eternal
Force driven by
Sweet melody
And meaning

Being,
What a potential
To tie all lose
Ends together,
Life after life…

Journey Beyond

Ah this
Unique being,
Who's a vibrant,
Exploding new ideas,
New opinions and
Ever spinning dreams

Let him
Pass through his
Time to grasp,
"Reality, *in Toto*"

Let his
Essence give
Strength to be
Relevant and

Let him
Travel through
The light,
"Who he is and
What he ought to be."

Force
That Binds

Religion be
Validated, if it
Preaches, "Universal
Compassion toward
All Humanity and

Leaving
No room
Either a forced
Conversion, or senseless
Violent claims"

Let each
Religion be relevant
To inspire the "Global
Spirit of goodwill"

Yes, let
Humanity
Coexists,
"In unity, equality
And peace with a
Sincerity of
A noble purpose"

Introspection

Time to
Erase, “Intellectual
Provincialism” as
The world is turning
Into a petite global
Village

Time to
Acknowledged
The Vedic thought
For its relevance with
Quantum and strings’
Interpretations coincides
Well

Time to
Reckon, “Dharma,
Karma, Tao, Filial Unity,
Ten Commandments,
Rahim and Nirvana…”

Being is the
Alive Universal
Ethical heritage;
Let him keep ascending…

Reflection

We must
Stand tall and be
The stubborn spirits
Of moral reason while
The rides on

Let us
Believe in our
Inner being and

Let our
Collective ethical will
Change the world for
Good

I mean,
Let us escape
From the sheer lunacy
Of bigotry, violence's'
And insane wars and
Be the real humans again…

Reciprocity

What if
There is a hidden
Reciprocity between
Known and the
Unknown?

What if,
Human doesn't
Understand such a
Logical connectivity,
How do we handle,
"His common sense,
Today"

Wonder,
Why being is the
Shadow beneath
His eternally
Lit-candle!

The Blueprint

Let us be
Guided by the
Moral reason and
Liberating us
From the thick layer
Of lies and greed

Let
The awakened
Souls get ready to
Make some good
Difference

Let each
Stands tall with
Courage and
Determined will to
Win the battle on hand

Let the
Logical necessity be
The blueprint ensuring,
"Thread that binds us
Shall enhance our collective
Meaning always."

Renaissance

Let's
Sing the song
Of our inner feelings
Before the world:

We're
The masters of
Our destiny, if we
Play the game well,
Of course

We've
Scan each page
Of history and mostly
It's mostly filled with
Many million deaths,
Destructions and
Miseries all right

What if
We confess our
Collective cruelty,
Arrogance and
Ignorance, and begin
To write new pages
In the name of our kids!

Love,
Eternal

Love,
What a reason
To live for

Love,
What a dream
To fight for

Love,
What a thrill to
Be

Hey girl,
In your
Smile, I feel love

In your
Laughter, I hear
Lyrics of the
Tender heart

Dear Heart,
You're
The meaning
Of my world, so
I ask,
"Please don't
Leave me ever again…"

Missing Variable

Beneath
The surface still
Conflicts and chaos
Prevails and
The mind never free
To point upward

Ideal thoughts
Always swirling, but
The execution is
Challenging, indeed

That is the
Reality of *sapiens*,
The wise and his
World still in
Eternal turmoil

Sorry, but the
Variables don't fit
Well in the
Set human equation…

Noble Path

Did you
Know, "Intellectual
Provincialism" is killing
The unity of our kind

Time is
Different today as
The world is rapidly
Turning into one petite,
"Global village"

Factional and
Tribal claims from
Varied "Isms" seem
Hazardous to the core
Of our essence

Let inspiring
Beings awakened to
Their moral call; lifting
Humanity along
A noble path called,
"Good."

Serendipity

Knowing,
"Life is so brief"
Why not, explore
And achieve the
Meaning of it in
Our time "

Is it not
A common sense
To listen and
Relearn, "How
To understand
One another?"

Is it not
Time to wake-up
To the new reality
Today and be ready
For tomorrow!

Come,
Let us regain our
Confidence,
"How to rise above
The cacophony, silly
Hang-ups and constant
Misery of the mind…

Covenant

If we
Want the world
To be a
Heavenly realm

In that case,
Each human be an
Expression of ethical
Action for certain

Not the talk,
But the walk is a
Necessity at every
Step to attain the
Mission

Let every
Sentient refrains
From his/her
Arrogance, ignorance
And indifferent attitude

Let us make it
Through the dark trail
Of death and destruction;
Leaving a noble legacy
To the young…

Infinity

Oh what a
Great riddle is
This cosmic
Being himself

He alone is
A metaphysical
Experience dancing
From death to death,
Ad infinitum

That is
The way I reckon,
The arduous journey
Of every intelligent
Being who's

Rolling
From one
Universe to another
And back and forth;
Not knowing,
"What is it all about?"

Irony of Fate

Intelligent
Human,
What a superb
Force of creative
Ideas and notions
Of the "Self" and
The reality around

He's been
Super busy
Unfolding every
Riddle; knocking
Off ignorance at
Every turning point

Alas,
Darkness still
Governs his mind;
Even when he's been
Walking through the
Illumined cosmos for
A very long…

Fulfillment

On seeing
You for the first time
I knew, our souls were
Locked-in for one
Spectacular journey
Forever

Yes,
That is when
Love spontaneously
Sparked while
Exchanging smile
For the first time

And, it's been
The same through
Our rough ride,
And am glad our
Dream turned into
Reality at once

Love,
What a miracle
Thread that gets
Stronger with trust
And time, indeed.

Blind Alley

Why
These recurring
Sins weakening the
Evolving being, time
After time

Why
These forces of
Darkness breeding
Pseudo-beliefs
And destructiveness,
Now and then

Why exists
In the world of
Uncertainty,
Mostly created by
The imperfect beings

Wonder,
Do us ever care
To know,
“Where’re we
Heading today?”

Touch-stone

We
Must be the
Lost techno-tribe,
Trying to lift our moral
Balloons to go up

I mean,
We're lost in this
Holistic reality of
Light and dark and

Don't know,
How to rescue our
Selves from recurring
Contradictions,
Paradoxes and
Hypocrisies of our time

Time to clear
The way for the
Balloons to kiss
"Perfection," and
Let us
Soar to the new heights
Of all possibilities…

Discovery

What
Am I real, or just
A mirage; dancing
In the reality that's
Completely unknown
To me!

What
Am I, just a lone
Voice in the totality
Of the whole universe,
Or what?

Let
I regain,
Clarity of all
This beauty and
Meaning; strengthening
My humanity, at once!

The Drama

In this
Cosmic complexity,
Life keeps
Blindly evolving
Either with a mission
Or simply aimlessly

Though in it,
Human is the major
Vision, vigor and a
Determined will, sadly
Fails to grasp his
Own relevance

Yes,
In this chameleon
Drama; he hasn't
Learn, "How to play
His role a hero"

Is he ever,
Trying to understand
His ethical existence
In it or not?"

Let it
Be the first
Question on the scene,
"What is the meaning to
Be a genuine human being?"

Being & Spirit

Who
Knows?
If am an image
In the mirror
Called, "I am.
I was. I shall."

Still,
Don't know, if
'Am driven by
My core
Essence or not

Let the
Spirit direct "I"
And silently reveal,
My real identity,
At once

Let "I"
Be the light flashing
Through the dark and
Be the awakened soul…

Big Question

Humanity,
What a prolonged
Dialogue to be

Its spinning
Time after time;
No completion of
The mission yet

Humanity,
What a ride to
Glorious blunders
And sins

That seems,
A sum total of
Our collective
Outcome as one
Divinely enterprise

Wonder,
"What legacy
Do we intend to
Leave behind?"

Ruminations

Every
Intelligent
Being striving to
Fulfill his dream

Every
Intelligent
Being asking:

"What is the
Meaning of him
Into this realm of
Uncertainty and
Subjective debates"

Why
Natural rhythm
Is calling to be
Calm and alert yet
He prefers to ignore?

And, why
Every searching
Spirit's struggling
So much to grasp,
"A simple Truth of
The self!"

Our Journey

It's
Always the
Same story,
"We never quit the
Blessed scene to prove
Our subjective point
Of view"

It's the
Ever rolling
Continuum; seeking
Complexity in otherwise
Simplicity no matter
What

That is
The tough journey
We've been on
Since our kind began
To reflect and seek
Understanding of
This half-evolved,
"Intelligent being…"

Being in Universe

If it is a
Dying universe,
Why we're in it for
There is no escape

Well then,
How do we
Measure freewill
Into such a
Deterministic fate

I mean,
"How dare do us
Even think; knowing
The truth of it all"

If it is a
Dying dream of
Of our hope,

"How
Do we justify
Our essence in such
A uncertain realm!"

Law of Life

Life
Dictates
Every born with
An equal dream
From
The beginning

When young,
That is the best
Time to make it
While
Holding right
Expectations
Of their set goals

Let them
Take charge;
Resetting the
Missing equation
From their elders and
Simply move on…

Contemplation

No matter
How one slices or
Dissects, in the final
Analysis,

"Being
Alone is answer in
Resolving the historic
Challenges and necessary
Changes in the name of
Good"

Being
Alone must assume
The responsibility;
Rejuvenating
Justice, beauty
And moral meaning

Yes, to his
Very existence or else
Hell shall loom over
His head forever…

Monkey Mind

It's been
Echoed many
Times before:

Lies and
Deceptions blur
The spiritual
Fidelity of every
Blessed being

Indeed, it's
The very enemy
Of his pursuit to
The moral will and
Truth

Don't let
Humanity keep
Sliding for there is
No escape, but to
Take responsibility;
Correcting the monkey
Mind…

Keep Marching

Keep
Marching on;
Holding all the
Big dreams you
Can

Keep
The spirit
Strong
While walking
Through the
Unknown trail

Remember,
Destination is
Quite a ways and
Still the
Steep mountains
To climb

Keep
The courage up
And be the master
Of your journey;
Pointing upward,
Every time…

Forever

Love,
Now that we've
Traveled so far,
Its time,

I express
My gratitude at
This very turning
Point

Soon,
We shall come
To a fork where
Life will bid us,
"Goodbye"

But don't
Worry our
Blended Souls
Shall continue
In eternity and

We shall
Be the
Truth forever,
Forever… forever…

Pensive

Sometimes,
I think,
"Reality, what a
Contradiction;
Challenging my
Mind
Time after time"

Sometimes,
I wonder,
"If we ever going
To regain humanity
Into one eternal
Unity or not?"

Sometimes,
I seek to know,
"Where're we
Heading?" either
Toward real joy or
Be stuck with the
Stubborn old grief!

Fragmented

Is being
An intelligent speck
Who's evolving through
Twelve dimensions of
The unknown reality or
What?

Or is he
A spiritual force
Moving through the
Self-assumption of
Being the seeker of
Truth or what?

Why these
Man-made notions:
Empirical vs
Metaphysical,
Good vs evil,
Relative vs absolute
And many more?

Why such
Synthetic complexities
When the logic insists,
"All is but a magnifique
Unity that yet to be
Understood well..."

Great Passage

Poetica,
Always the
Best expression;
Emanating from
The core of my
Essential being

Poetica,
What a meditative
Experience; lifting
My "Freewill"
Every time

Poetica,
What a creative
Thread bonding
My humanity with
Others

Let it
Keep rolling and
Let it catapult, "I"
To the clarity of that
Waiting Truth…

Life is Funny

And we
Shine and dine
While
All that keeps
Rolling on

Yes, while we
Dream and dance
We end up in an
Unknown realm

It's true,
We fight for
A good name,
And keep walking
While holding our
Noble goals

When in
Love with
Many dreams,
We're
Not sure, if we
Shall make it or
Not?

Time
To Spark

Despite
Surface
Differences,

All hearts are
Throbbing at
Equal
Frequencies of
Hope and love

That's been
The latent force;
Keeping the global
Spirit on

That's the
Inner spark still
Keep us sane and

That's why
Existence seems
Quite
Meaningful and
Full of goodwill even
In the dark…

Morning Stroll

What an
Inspiring morning
In this stunning
Sunny place

Where
The Blue Sea
Keeps kissing the
Terra endless

What a
Refreshing is
The scenery where
Nature and I are
But One

What a
Wonderful is the
Beauty of such an
Awakened place

Where
'Am fully immersed
Into these roaring
Mighty waves…

Let's Be Human

Hiding
Beneath the pile of
Ignorance yields
Nothing but
Misery and tears,
To say the least

Not a
Smart way to lead
Life that has so much
To give in return

Did you
Ever think of
Children,
"How they'll live
In the world of fear,
Uncertainty and
Greed!"

Did you
Ever care to
Think of your
Fate in their
Place?

The Spirit

It's
A crazy
World where
'Am either lost or
Found; now and
Then

Love too,
Where
'Am caught
Between right or
Wrong always

In it all,
"I" seems to be
Walking Choice
Machine; carrying
The full load of
Dreams and goals

Alas, 'am
Running short of
Time while on a
Long arduous
Unknown highway
Of my Truth to be…

What's The Point!

Being
Wrapped-up
Into the milieu
Of his turmoil
And broken
Dreams

Wonder,
"What's the point?
When death equals
All the differences
In the end

I mean,
What's the fuss?
"Who's wise and
Who's not?" when
Humanity still rots
With tears and
Double-talks

Wonder,
"What's the point?
Being in a hurry to
Make the name when
Destined
To die at anytime…

Fortitude

Life got a
Meaning; what
You can do today

Life got a beauty
And truth, if you can
Begin the real journey,
At once

Let you
Be a creative
Adventure; leading
From known to the
Unknown through
Integrity of the mind

Yes,
Let you roll
From imperfection
Toward perfection
And let you be the
First awakened soul
From the slumbering
Lot …

Loves Destiny

Sweet Heart,
Let me give
All that I have to
Make you happy
Every more

Sweet love,
Forgive my
Petite blunder, but
No way to hurt
Your heart

Come, my life
Let me touch
Your soul and in
Return just say,
"I love you too!"

Dear Heart,
For us, there is
Neither a beginning
Nor any end to it at all…

Our Reality

While holding
Onto our hearts,
We keep
Walking through
Shifting sands of
Life and time

We keep
Staring at the blue
Sky and drink the
Love from it all

All the
Swirling winds
Kicking us now
And then,

But we
Stand together
Against million odds,
And still standing tall
On the terra firma,
"Mutual trust and
Nothing but the trust."

Only
For You

I say,
Life got the
Meaning for your
Love's so deep and
True

Yes,
Sweet Soul,
Your smile's a
Heavenly feelings
Giving lot of
Hope to dream

Sweet Life,
"Don't run away
From the path
We've built it for
A long "

I say it again,
"Come back and
Be the person, I
Knew before..."

Fearless Bird

Like that
Fearless
Majestic bird;
Flying so high
In the mighty
Blue skies

Let
I fly high above
From the senseless
Bleeding world
Where greed, falsity
And the turmoil is
Killing billion dreams

Like that
Pure free bird,
Let I roam my world
With such a calm and
Self-confident way;
Lifting all my humanity
To the highest point…

Nothing So New

When
A Soul bids,
"Goodbye, all the
Causes and consequences
Ceases; only nothingness
Fills the left over void"

Well,
They claimed after
Many millennia,
"Universe is not real!"
Not a big surprise

It's just
An echo from the
Vedic past stating,
"Real and unreal" is
The matter of one's
Consciousness

That is either
It's "Saguna," the
World of attributes
Or one without
Called, "Nirguna."

Our Time

When the
Guardians are
Governed by the
Evil forces;

Only
Deaths and
Destructions are
The inevitable
Consequences

That is
What the world
History informs
Us, time after time,

But human
Memories fail
Each time and the
Cycle keeps recurring,
Ad infinitum

Funny, in this
"Age of Info, we still
Remain illiterate and
Quite arrogant while
Ignoring the same old
Bloody history…"

Dear Lady

Lady,
Yes my dear
Lady, it's a
Pleasure being
With you

Lady,
In you, there is
My world with
You

Let life
Keeps rolling
While we keep
Singing;
The splendid
Love lyrics

Yes,
Dear lady,
All is sweet and
Shining while
We keep dancing
Cheek to cheek,
Forever…

Welcome

Welcome
To my world where
Our dream is waiting
To say, "Hello"

Hey babe,
It's time to dance
And be merry from
Here to eternity

Welcome
To our common
Destiny and be in
Love forever

I say, "Be
Brave
And make the
First move"

For our
Dream is waiting
To say,
"Hello, again"

Ascension

I am
Not here when
Tranquility
Governs my spirit
Either now or never

I am best
When Nature
Is the sole
Harmony and
Inspiration to my
Solemn soul

Let I silently
Roam through
Every wonder
Of life and time
While my rides on

That's the
Spirit of my joy
That's the
Triumph of my
Essence for sure…

Splendor Of Truth

Without
Transition from
Impurity of the mind
To the enlightenment

There is
No way, can I climb
The steep mountains
That're so high

It's about,
"Progression,
Progression and
Progression, at all
The time"

Let it be the
Norm and let I keep
Evolving through it
Always

No exception
Whatever the
Temptations… let
Life flow with best
Intention and goodwill…

Being & Meaning

Self,
What a
Splendid
Riddle to be

While
Roaming
Through the
Zigzag trail of
Myriad
Uncertainties

In such a
Complexity,
Discovery of
The Self, always
A splendor of truth

Let the
Self endeavor
Be the magnificent
Quest of all and
Nothing else….

The Bliss

Scintillating
Thoughts keeps
Rebuilding a new
Vision at every
Turning point

And there is
Serendipity as I
Flip new pages of
My life and time

All set
Patterns
Everywhere and
Everything keeps
Renewing
On their own

In it,
"I" must
Emerge as a
Ultimate meaning
On the scene…

Decoded

Come,
Let's ride the
Future for it
Determines the
Past

What is called,
"Retro-causality"
To honor the
Notion at this
Time

Yes,
Let's awaken
The soul to grasp
Simplicity within
And move on
Toward the future

Let's change
Attitude and bring
Clarity and harmony
As the best prize
While we're willing to
Transform at this
Time …

Sakshi

(The witnessing Consciousness)

Oh that
Sacred sound,
"OM, OM, OM…"
From the super massive
Black hole keeps buzzing
The Universe since the
Inception

What an
Amazing coincidence
Between Vedic "Brahman,
The witnessing consciousness"
And the quantum conclusion

All finite
Consciousness, albeit
"Atamans" is projection of
The Eternal Consciousness,
"Brahman;"
The mystical thread that
Bind all differences into One

That is the
Crux of a parallel
Insight of the Vedic wisdom
And the modern scientific
Quest still in-progress called,,
"Theory of Everything"

Admonition

It must be
The mind that is
Buried beneath
Thick pile of,

“Ignorance,
Pride and
Prejudice,”
What a biggest
Disease of the
Intelligent beings

To achieve
The waited,
“Human Greatness,”
Time to erase the
Old habits as soon
As we must

Our grand
Story is but a few
Brief moments
Of peace, and
Many millions
Death in-between,
“What a pity indeed?”

Miracle, Or Curse!

Wonder
Where the future
Is taking us

Now we're
Going to throw
Insect spy drones
Tied-up with camera
And microphone

They can
Maneuver through
Any tiny space and
Even can suck DNA,
To steal our identities;
On the spot

That's the
Scary nano-tech
Magic still in its
Embryonic state

But, the
Wheels are into
Motion as we keep
Moving far beyond the
Orwellian imagination!

Liberation

What if,
It's not the Great
Divine, but we're the
"First Cause" of all
Our collective troubles

Well, history
Backs up the fact of
The stated issue that
We all know it so well

Why
Not then understand
The very root cause of
Our lasting plight

Why not
Go to the source
And lift off the
Pseudo-tale, and be
The enlightened beings…

Walk the Walk

Life got the
Meaning all right;
It's the human
Who s must know,
"Truth on their own"

If we all
Wake-up in time
With such a simple
Common sense; we
May be already
Strolling along and

Get ready
To walk the walk
And explore the
"Individual,
Core Essence."

Bold Necessity

Looking
At the confused
And violent world

Why
Abandon
The meaning and
Objectivity of our
Moral will?

I mean,
When
Humanity is
Threatened by
Fear & uncertainty

"Why run
Away from our
Collective social
Responsibility,
At this very time?"

Great Ride

While
On a carousal ride,
I keep
Wondering, "What
If we're not real in this
Make belief realm?"

What if it is a
One giant dream;
Swirling us through
"Life-Death cycles"

Perhaps, it's
Another brief ride
And nothing else

Whatever
It may be, let's just
Seize the experience
Before another dream
Flashes our images over
The holographic screen…

The Flow

So the world
Flows forward by
The nano-sec

And all seems
Silently evolving
Toward
Moral fortitude

The path is
Well defined,
Why human is
Not rolling along
That right track

Why
Human is lethargic
And shying away
From the
Spiritual perfection,
He aspires to be!

Being & Truth

We're
Contextual
Wandering spirits;
Trying to understand
This holistic reality
Before our times up

In such a
Scenario, our
Destiny is threaded
With anxiety, fear
And endless dreams

Only way
We shall survive is
To drop the divisional
Mentality at once

Time to
Reckon, fragility of
Our kind in this milieu
Of uncertainty, of course

Let's simply
Relearn,
"How to be friends
And build a better world
For the children's sake..."

Affirmation

We
Pursue
Unknown every
Day through
Many different
Ways

We
Explore zillion
Stars in this vast
Universe

And often,
We forget
To introspect,
“Who we’re and
What we
Ought to be”

In doing so,
We ignore our
Truth, “We’re
The center of all
Possibilities…”

Everyman's Song

I am birth,
I am life and
I am death and
I spin forever,
"Becoming,"
Each time

I think,
I am intentional
Who's driven by
Million crazy dreams
And desires I can hold

Why
Don't I then
Leave the hedonistic
Life and be ready to
Have a disciplined
Mind!

Why am I
Such a helpless victim
Of these out dated tales?

Dancers

Did we
Ever know,
"We've been dancing
Into the fire for a
Very long"

It's all
Energies revolving
With different shapes
And forms from macro
To the micro scales

To that
We call it, "Our
Reality that is in
Constant flux"

We're the
Dancers gathered
To be in harmony
Of our souls

Let this
Grand fire of
Cremation after
Cremation keep purifying
Every corrupted soul…

The Curse

We haven't
Yet mopped-up
The historic mess

It's still
A mountain high
Pile of struggles
And tears

Is it okay?
To keep breathing
Dirty air, drinking
Polluted water and
Eating the junk
Food!

No wonder,
Obesity, diabetes
And high stresses;
Rising every where

Wonder,
What is "Progress?"
When humanity is not
Healthy and happy
At any time!

Sometimes

Sometimes,
What I hear from
The cosmic hymns
Is the Beginning
Of a new meaning;
Defining our destiny
To be

Sometimes,
I fall back
And try again
To take charge of
The trail 'am on to
Reach the sanctum
Of the Self-truth

At each
Turning point,
I must take
A stand against the
Tide of change, if
There is no moral
Strength in it

Sometimes,
I stand alone and
Reshape my thoughts
Over and again to
Remember those
Sacred Vedic hymns…

Force
To Be

Why be
Afraid of the
Cruel world and
Run away from
It all

When
We can
Direct reality
Through our
Choices and deeds

Why be
An embodiment
Of grief and guilt
And be in despair

When
We're
The masters
Of our destiny

Albeit,
We're the force
Who can conquer
Their mind and be free…

Timeless

What a
Fascination
At the first sight;
Shaking-up my
Inner being so much

Your
Awesome beauty,
Dimples and the
Smile; capturing
My heart forever

"That was,
That is…that shall"
And I will cherish
Your lovely face
All through

I know
You're laughing
And thinking, "What
Kind of fool am I,
"Who silently adores
Your heart so much!"

Stand Tall

Please
Don't delay the
Walk while the
Time is slipping
Away so fast

I say,
"Don't live off
With false promises
And shallow beliefs
For there is not enough
Time left to delete them"

Be in time
To restore your
Predious humanity,
Dignity and moral
Reality for sure

And be the
Winner of your
"Freewill," to the
Very end as well…

Glow In Dark

I think,
We're
Born to be the
Winners no matter
What

And at times,
I fall back and
Think otherwise
When 'am in my
Despair

Always it's
Existence
Seems to be the
Last chance

Where
"I got to be the
Free will who dares
To take a giant leap
Forward…

Essence

"I,"
Just an ordinary
Human species
Who's a living sum
Total of
Million memories
And experiences

"I," just
An insignificant
Flare from the mighty
Fiery Universe; seeking
My truth only

Though 'am
Finite, I got the guts
To think and know
"Who am I and
What's my worth?

You bet,
'Am an ever struggling
Flame; flickering in the
Winds of this enigmatic
World that's on fire
Fortoo long…

Turbulence
To Tranquility

Where
Separation
Of the self
From all others is
The main theme

There begins
A big dance of
Subjectivity, and
Many questions
Take hold on the
Battlefield

Once beyond
Fragmented world
Of chaos and
Complexity, unity
Got to be the
Supreme conclusion

Time to
Begin a new journey
Time to
Seek the ultimate
Destiny, and be free…

Pre-Requisites

This is
Our time,
This is
Our chance

This is the
Turning point
Let's not
Delay the walk

For life is
Short and the
Trail too long

Yes,
We need to act,
We need to heal,
We need to
Change, in return…

Beware

No matter,
How a few big
Boys claim

To justify
The super AIs
And their clones

In fact,
They are silently
Killing our
Freedom

Don't forget
The "Orwellian
Ghost" and

Don't forget
The future of
Our kids, please…

Revival

Why
Don't we climb
Over the
Great Wall of
Ignorance and be
Free

Why
Wait so long
Into the cage of
Falsity, deception
And lies

I mean,
"How long do
We tolerate this
Myopic state of
The mind?"

Why
Don't we
Strengthen our
"Global Spirit,"
And move on…

Anniversary, Everyday

Your
Everlasting love
Opened up the
Entire spectrum of
All possibilities

Yes,
Dear heart we've
Triumphant the long
Journey together and
Still more dreams to
Roll on

That got
To be the awesome
Power of our trust
And commitment

That got
To be the Thread
That kept us bonded
Together so long…

The Gist

Behind
The veil,
There is
Nothing but a
Demand for
Truth only

For being
Alone defines,
Existence via
His logical
Necessity to
Understand,
"All That Is"

That seems
To be the gist of
His intellectual
Journey

That seems
To be the core of
His moral essence,
Indeed…

The Mirror

What a
Fascination of this
Celestial paradise
Called,
"Human Creativity"
Where "Perfection"
Governs the mind,
Always

In such an
Inspiring milieu;
Eternally evolving
Dream transforms
Into reality all right

Indeed, that is
Where happiness is
Woven with harmony
And hope

In other
Words let illumined
Souls be the real
Expression of the
Magnifique Universe…

New Journey

As I
Take off from
The world,
I bid,
Avoir to
All that was, that is
And that shall be
As my legacy behind

No string
Attached, but the
Journey was my
Struggle to seek,
"Love, Truth and
To be a moral being"

As I pass
Through eternity,
I have become
Light, light…light
Everywhere and 'am
No more but a sheer
Nothingness at the
Same time!

To Be

Optimistic
Folks offer the force
Of positive change

They're the
Sherpa's climbing
Over the steepest
Slopes

Oh how
Lucky, the world's
Been to bring out
Such heroes,' time
After time

Let their
Number increase
And let the collective
Glow of humanity
Continues, life after
Life

Let
Children stay
Smiling with their
Dreams, life after
Life…

Facilitator

It's been
Said million times,
"Consciousness is
The real engine"

That gives
Humans to know
And understand their
Reality ever"

Indeed,
We humans are
The object of
Consciousness and
That's the passage to
Know the final truth

No point
Ignoring the simple
Fact of our essence,
And no point
Avoiding the issue
On-hand

"What is our
Meaning into this
Spinning sphere of
Uncertainty after all!"

That's Love

Love,
What gives is
A spirit of
Mental toughness

It's in love,
We're the lyrics of
Best of joys and
Worst of grief's

In life,
We struggle
To win the best
Dream when in
Love with another
Caring soul

Love
What a Sharpe
Two-edged sword,
Always hanging over
Every lover's head…

Still on The Trail

Still don't
Know,
"Who we were,
Who we are or
Who we shall"

That's the
Unknown path,
We're on

Either
The question is
Right or

The answer
Is correct that
Still unknown

That's the
Trail we've been
Walking for a long;
Not knowing where
We're heading?

Be Inspired

We've
Freedom
To choose and
Whatever soothes
Our logical necessity
To fulfill

We fall in
Love with other
Who holds special
Feelings and willing
To walk the walk
For a long

We admire
All noble heroes
For their moral stand
Who never changes
Their track, no
Matter what may be
The consequence

Let us
Emulate such heroes,
And be worthy humans;
What we ought to be…

The Quest

Why don't
We begin the walk
Toward purification
Of our collective sins

Yes,
Why don't we
Erase the old habits
Of deaths and
Destructions at once

Though
The journey is
Challenging, we've no
Choice, but to roll
Toward that
Set Noble Goal

Time to
Act together now
Before our children's
Future is no more…

Peel Off Illusion

Not the
Great Divine,
But human alone got
To be the master of his
Unresolved issues

Not just
The prayers,
But the courage and
Integrity of the mind
Be the forward
Thrust is best

Not what the
Preacher says, but
To be a moral courage
Himself matters the most

Not what
The experts says,
"What to do and
How to…"doesn't
Mean much,

But the
Collective endeavor
To do good is the
Meaningful outcome…

Fearless

Nothing
Seems
To be surety:
Not life, not death,
Not love, not even
Truth itself

Yet
Humans keep
Walking through
Prayers and rituals
To meet their wish

Perhaps,
There is something
Beyond that keeps
Them evolving
Through the dark
Patches of existence…

Unsettled

Being
Living in
The world of
Many dimensions

He
Understands
All that is via
Perceptuality,

But then
It's just a
Half-the-journey
To the Temple of
Full reckoning

Well the
Consequential
Being, suffers
And struggles while
Debating ever

Let him
Takes charge and
Let grasp his meaning
In this wild charade…

Spontaneity

Let
Spontaneous
Insight be the
Way to grasp
Melody, rhythm
And the meaning
Of it all

Let
Serendipity,
Open the
Inner being and
Let it conquer
The mind itself

Let
Human be
The pure essence
Of love, truth,
Right vision and
Moral inspiration

Let such an
Awakened human
Be the reality of
Children's dream,
Too…

The Code

Each
Individual, a
Moral substance,
What a
Precious gift

Each
Engaged in
Defining his/her
Worldview

Each a
Cause and
Consequence of
His/her deed

Each
To be free
From guilt and
Grief

Each
To make it
Through on their
Own…

Take Note

A belief is
A failed enterprise,
If it lacks compassion
Toward the whole

A belief is
A failed mission,
If it promotes death
And destruction

A belief is
A failed pursuit,
If it is driven by
Dogmatic claims and
Refuses to reform

A belief is
Invalidated, if it
Instigates blood spills
And wars

A belief is
A liability to the
World, if it forces
Its narrative over
Others either through
Coercion or fraud…

Moral Reference

A few
Flashing thoughts
About the being
To be

Let
Each be worthy
To attain the ideals
Of virtue,
Par excellence

Let
Each be the
Courage;
Lifting others to
The equal height

Let
Each be the
Aesthetic beauty
And a superbly
Aware Soul to
Measure up to the
Moral reference…

Paradise

It's a
Beautiful day
To celebrate

While
Basking
Under the Sun,
Fun and sand,

Yes, in this
Grand State of
Million flowers;
Where folks
Keep smiling
Every whichever
Way

Let
Each passing
Moment be their
Heavenly
Experience

I say,
"Let 'em
Keep enjoying,
Even life may be
A chaotic harmony,
Every day…"

The Grasp

It is
Incumbent
Upon each of us

Let the
Self conquer its
Original “Identity”
And move on

Let it
Refine for good
To hold our
Big dreams

Let it
Redefine the
Connectivity
With new dawn

Let the
Self arise, and
Be a fearless;
Smashing through
All irrational “Isms,”
And the pseudo-
Claims…

Each Step

When
We believe,
We begin to explore

When
We explore,
We begin to discover

And
We tie the
Thread with all the
Unknowns in time

So we
Ascend; justifying
Our essence, our
Existence and our
Will to win

That is
The nature and
Scope of every, "I"
While walking
Through shifting
Sands of a sealed
"Hour-Glass…"

Sinners & Victims

I hear,
Lovers singing
Through tough
Times

I see,
Them holding
Hands; trying
To stand tall

I see,
Soldiers caught
In a bloody war;
Trying to be alive

I hear,
Children trapped
In a senseless war;
Shattering their
Beautiful Dreams,
So soon!

Synergy

What if,
Obsession of
“Facts;”
Undermines our
Journey beyond!

Let there
Be a
Complimentarily
Between reason
And spiritual insight

Let
Empirical mind
Be connected to
Metaphysical to see
The two sides of
Truth

Let
Every mind
Emanate the
Very meaning of
Existence and fly
Off the edge…

Back off

Come
Let us enhance,
"Universal Idea of
Unity and dignity
Of humanity, first"

Let the
Pious servants
Stop preaching
For a change

Let the
"Global Spirit of
Love" be the
Dominant narrative

Let
Guardians refrain
From launching
Insane wars, now and
Then and

Let the
Common folks,
Enjoy their gift of
Peace and life itself
From this point on…

Best Lovers

Now that
We're one
Blended soul

Shall we
Sing and dance
To salute meaning
Of you and I

Shall we,
Fly over the
Trouble times and
Be the winners of
Our life and time

Come,
Dear heart and
Let's rewrite the
Story and be in
Love forever…

A View

Beyond
Ignorance and
Violence,
There is
A place called,

“Awakening with
Noble thoughts,
Words and deeds”

Let us
Dare go beyond
Bickering, debates
And confusions

Come, let us
Tackle the main
Issue,
“Who we’re and
What we ought
To be…”

Beware

Why don't
We seek
Genuine identity
In this
Fast changing
Realm

Where
AIs and
Millions smart
Machines are
Blatantly
Controlling
Our freedom

Why don't
We wake-up
Registering our
Collective protest

Why
Guardians are
Empty handed with
Their legislative
Measures

Why such
A timid response?
Why such despicable
Apathy?

Off
The Cage

When
All explanations
Begin and end
With irrational
Defense

There
Eventually
Emerges, the call
To rid off all the
Lingering
Contradictions
And pseudo-claims

When
Each tribe is
Pushing its geographic
God to the insane
Extreme

Wonder,
"What is the
Universal meaning,
"Omniscient,
Omnipotent and
Omnipresent?"

Half-Way

Rational
Thinking begins
With a premise

In that case,
It's logically
Incumbent upon us
To open the path:

"The First Cause,"
"Eternal Essence" or
Simply something else

Even, modern
Scientists too are
Probing through the
Lenses of quantum,
Strings and some
Waiting unknowns

What if,
Human still is a
Half-way evolved
Awareness then

How shall we
Claim, "We know
The Truth and we've
Ended the mission..."

Open-up

Time
To roll-up
The sleeves and
Begin
Measuring depth
Of our
Commitments

I mean,
Be in action
Through
Moral courage
To arrive at the
Gate of boldness

Let us
Wake-up to
The truth,
For we're
Failing to adapt
New reality today

Yes, we've
Responsibility for
The future of children
Let us at least act
On their behalf today…

Ramifications

Quantum
Logic
Opened-up the
Mind to drop the
Notion, "The
Absolute certainty"

There is
But probability and
Randomness defining,
"All there is"

That is a
Great turning
Point; freeing us
From the surety of
Anything perhaps
The divine himself!

Let
The Intelligent
Beings begin to
Understand, "How
Their reality keeps
Expanding without
Any certainty…"

Twists & Turns

Why don't
Billion silent souls
Reverberate the
Mighty Universe

Why don't
Billion folks come
Together and take a
Bold stand

Why don't
We quit the ugly
Scene of
Daily deaths
And discontent

Why don't
We open-up and
Be friends and not
The crazy strangers;
Be the meaningful
Human beings…

Being & Perfection

Goodwill
Up wells benign
Thoughts and
Action always

Creativity
Emanates
Deep curiosities
Of the unknown

Love
Stays steady with
The thread that bind
Two honest souls
Forever

Awakening
Arises the
Optimistic heroes
From darkness

For truth is
The moral essence;
Energizing a few
Optimistic heroes…

Conditional Journey

As we
Keep walking
Through the
Long journey

Our
Collective dreams;
Must be in harmony
With one another

It would be
Our Herculean
Strength enabling
To beat million odds

We'll have
To remain calm and
Rational every time

Again, we'll
Have to dismiss all
The dogmatic claims to
Make the journey through…

Let Go

Let go
Bad memories
Of yesterday's

Let go
Revenge, and
Be free
From the jaws
Of ignorance

Let go
The historic evil
And be sure;
Never happens
Again

Enough
Of endless asinine
Blunders and sins
To know

Its time,
To move on for a
Greater good of the
Whole today and
Now…

Voyagers

Our voyage
Through the rough
Sea is a constant
Uncertainty

Our ships
Being
Hurled by the
Giant rogues yet
It never sank

Well, the
Ships quite tough
So are
Humans aboard
As well

Against
The entire killer
Turbulences;
Nature remaining
So calm

Let's be
Inspired by her
Awesome resilience
And be the
Winners at last...

Jewel

Hey she's just a
Perfect corporate
Gal

I mean, she's
A very impressive
Flare and her names,
"Jewel"

Every
Time she enters
The headquarter,
All bosses get down
To her knees

They keep
Wondering, "Hey,
Very sassy gal,
What's on your
Mind today?"

Hey,
The shining
Jewel of every
Curious heart,
"What do you
Intend to do next!"

Sentient

We
Keep jumping
From
One unknown
To another, and

Not
Knowing where
The destiny is
Evolving

Yes, we
Keep on
Querying,
"Why life passes
Away so quickly"

Let mind
Be calm and
Let's fall back
For a while and

Let us
Measure our
Collective moral
Strength to take the
First step…

Quintessence

Perfect
Beauty defines
Solemn souls
Pure essence

That is
When human
Is an awakened
And his
Journey begins
In earnest

Let each
Human be such
A quintessential
Difference maker

Yes,
The world needs
Such transformational
Moral giants today
Than ever…

Some Issues

Reality
May be
A long term dream;
Granting enough time
First to wonder
And then comprehend
All that is unknown

Perhaps,
Existence is
A hidden code
Yet to be deciphered
From one generation
To another or what?

Are we
Lost time travelers
Who hasn't understood:
The melody, the lyrics and
It's meaning thus far!

Missing

Stubborn
Will to
Understand
Truth got to be
The mother of all
Human endeavors

If so,
Why stand still
And not have the
Courage to walk
Through darkness
At any time

Meanwhile
When AIs are
Slowly taking charge
Under the disguise of
"Progress"

Why do we
Stand still ignoring
The death of our
Freedom so soon!

Will to Believe

Thoughts, words
And deeds define
Our destiny all right

In that case,
Let our
Existential intention
Be nothing more than,
"Awakening,"

Let's get
The grip over our
Misconceptions and
Let's seek
Freedom from the
Cultish claims

Let's
Go beyond the
Closed sphere and
Regain,
Our dignity, our
Humanity, at one…

End Game

Intelligent
Beings flying
Off the edge;

Pursuing
Meaning to
Their existence

Whatever
Subjective
Values they may
Hold, but

The purity
Of their essence
Remains

That's the
First hint, they
Are relevant
Indeed…

No Escape

No matter
What but God
Is always one,
Save for the
Corrupt mind of
The zealots

That is
The irony of
Ignorant beings
Who never
Understood such
A simple common
Sense

Sadly,
In the ever
Changing locations
Of the Great Divine;
Many millions were
Killed and

Still many
Dying today, and the
Beat goes so silently…

The Thread

We had
Men wearing
Different hats:
Logical positivists,
Skeptics, Cynics,
Subjective beliefs
And many more

They brought
Nothing, but more
Debates, conflicts
And confusions in
Return

They stalled
The forward
Possibilities:
Unity, beauty and
Humanity to be

It's in
Tranquility,
Where authentic
Human must awake,
And be the thread
Of all lose ends…

Direction

If we're
Alone in this
Ever exploding
Universe

Is it not
A *prima facies*,
"We're a distinct
Distillation of Truth
To be understood"

And if we're
Alone to think and
Explore many
Unknowns

In that case,
"Don't we've a
Hidden mission,
Yet to be unveiled"

Let it be
The first clarity
Before launching
The journey toward
Our meaning…

Awakening

Man
Always a
Creature of the
Old habits

Whose
Moving
At snail speed
While the world
Flies so fast

No wonder,
His moral vigor
Wanes; leaving
Ignorance behind

Time
To wake-up from
The nightmare and
Kill the old habits,
At once

Time to
Understand. It's
Time to move on…

Thrust Forward

Don't be
Distressed while
Walking through the
Patch of darkness

Don't
Struggle too much.
Don't despair, but be
Calm and be alert

Don't forget
To ask always,
'What is the
Meaning of you
In the totality of
All it is?"

I say,
"Get-up and go
After your dreams,
And never be
Distressed again…"

Be Confident

Don't you
Worry, what
Others may
Think or say,
Just keep the
Ride going

For you're
Reality of your
Reason and
The holder of
Your judgment,
Indeed

Let your
Illumined spirit
Take charge and
Let you ignore
The bad mouths

Let you
Keep walking to
The noble goal and
Never give a damn,
"What others
May think or say…"

Adaptability

Wise
To give credit
To the will
Over intellect

For will is
Real power;
Propelling toward
Unity always

If you're
On a wrong trail,
Change it before
It's too late

Be a new,
"Soul Force" and
Reach the sanctum
Of your truth

Let the
Will help you
Conquer the mind
And be free forever…

Fortitude

When
Dark clouds keep
Looming over the
Head

Just take a
Deep breath and
Let the spirit
Awaken with calm

Let
Your moral being
Lift you above and
Make you grasp,

"There is an
Eternal
Beauty in the
Universe and
That is you're"

Don't ever
Disturbed by the
Trivial things…just
Stay focus and beat
The dark clouds…

Renewal

The collective
Hope of one
Humanity must
Stand tall

In knowing,
"Our differences
With sane mind,
Will transformed us
Into greatest unity
Of all"

That is the
First opening.
Yes, that is the
First ascension;
Leaving a right
Legacy behind

Time to
Drop the rotted
Historic roots and
Let young begin the
Journey with a
New spirit of unity
And mutual trust…

Magic, It Is

Only in
Romance,
We're
Perfection of
Our souls

Only in
Romance, love
Shall grow ever,
Ever, ever, ever…

Yes,
Sweet Heart,
That is our truth
And that is our
Destiny in motion

Of course,
Of course
That is the glory
Of our two
Blended hearts
Forever, forever…
Forever…

The Vibes

Loves
The thread
Binding all

Loves
The music
Ringing it all

Just
Learn to
Extend friendship
And win the world

Be
Happy and
Believe in the self
And keep rolling

I say,
Keep going and
Keep singing the
Love song and be the
Winner to the end…

Big Leap

Let's
Open-up our
Ever inspiring
Future where
Humanity keeps
Renewing at all time:

New ideas,
New attitude
Reshaping;
New worldviews
Now and then

Let's
Learn to discover
You and I and let's
Relearn to listen to
One another

While
Building
One beautiful
Humanity, "Soul
To Soul..."with calm
And alert all right…

Excelsior

When
Shall there
Be time
To know,

"The sentient
Is the embodied
Good at the core"

When
Shall we be the
Movers of our true
Colors and

Paint the
World as one
Beauty forever

When
Shall billion
Hearts, minds
And Souls be

Awakening,
Real meaning of
Us at the very core …

"I"

"I"
Prompts
To go
After what
Best therc is

"I,"
What a
Transformational
Journey of the
Spirit

"I"
What a
Human miracle
Exploring the self
And the world ever

"I,"
An eternal
Reverberation of
Endless curiosities
Resonating between
Birth and death,
Essentially…

Finite to Infinite

Humanity
Remains best
When generation
After generation
Keeps the candle lit

As the
Story evolves,
Let clarity of our
Essence be grasped
Across the board
To meet the set goal

Let
It be known,
"Each is a finite
Awareness destined
To define meaning,
All the way to the end…"

Moral Will

In its
Pure sense,
Humanity be
A manifest
Moral will;
Justifying our
Existence

Let it be
The prime
Principle to take
The first step

Come,
Time to
Understand,
“Who we’re and
What we can
Become”

That be the
Path, the
Rationale and the
Noble Mission while
The journey is on…

The Awakened

Seeing
Three sights of
Suffering:
Old age,
Disease body and
Death

Gautama's
Life changed and
Made him the first
Optimistic
Existentialist and
Who later known,
"Buddha" to the
World

He
Understood the
Very essence of
Humans; asking
To follow the
Eight Noble paths
And be free from
The trivial *Dukhas*…

Noble Worth

Faith,
Be personal and
No middle man in this
Noble Experience of
Every being

Truth,
Be the light of
Every individual;
Discovered on his/her
Own

Love,
Be the throbbing
Pulses of every
Lover who cares
And trusts the
Other caring heart

Being,
What an ever
Dynamic adventure
Powered by
Boldness, creativity
And moral will…

Resilience

Nobody
Can win
The battle of
Perfection, but the
Determined will can

Nobody
Can threaten our
Freedom, but
Our collective sin can

Nobody
Should doubt,
“We’re the
Ascending Spirits
Against the tide of
Million defeats…”

Let us be
Bold and be the
Single voice,
“We’re the
Masters of our
Common destiny, and
We’re never afraid…”

Invention!

Hell is
Invention of our
Misdeeds and false
Judgments

That is
How our struggles
Began and that is
What we're facing
Today

The hell is
Very anxiety and
Fear of day to day
Existence

The hell
Is our greed
Driven corruption,
Blood spills and
And senseless decisions

The hell
Creators may be
Few in numbers;
Controlling our minds;
So quietly all right!

Steep-Climb

It's been
Questioned
Many
Times before,
"What if
Religious doses
Been fatal to the
Believers or what?"

It's been
Written by a few
Big thinkers,
"What if we're
Born sinners," and
Asking,
"To get off the
Deep hole before
We may not…"

It's been
Sang by many
Lovers,
"Whether they
Can make it through
The stormy time of
Their struggles and
Despair or not!"

Juggernaut

Society,
What an incredible
Amalgamation of
Collective consciousness;
Often running
Aimlessly without
Knowing the futuristic
Consequences

Society,
Always a ceaseless
Flow of humanity either
Ascending or descending;
At every
Historic turning point

Society,
What a juggernaut force
Of love and hate, despair
And hope…right and wrong;
Blindly evolving toward
An unknown

Society,
Where billion egos and
Dreams colliding; resulting
Sometimes into beauty and
Truth and sometimes just
A greed driven arrogance
And insane wars…

Subjective Being

Mind,
A magic that's eternally
In flux where everything
Spinning with many million
Thoughts

It's a
Loadstone embedded
With subjective queries,
Contradictions and
Paradoxical conclusions,
Many times

Mind,
Always a revolving
Wheel of creativity,
Curiosity… flirting with
The teasing truth

Mind,
An ever evolving
State of the being keeps
Exploding and at times,
Retarding while passing
Through the endless
Uncertainties and dreams …

The Stigma

Oh the
Bad days of the
Colonial sins

Imposed
In the name of
Cruelty, greed and
False superiority of
Their evil minds

Perhaps,
It was the disease
Caused by the crazy
"Ethnocentrism" and

The disease
Was inflicted by
The false assumption,
"Survival of the fittest"

Well, nothing,
Divinely good happened,
But the deeply wounded
Humanity still bleeding in
Many places today…

Conquer The Dream

Let
Every Soul soar
Like a noble candor
And got it's
"Bird's Eye View"

Where
Splendor of
Truth is blooming
Everywhere in the
Greenery of Nature

And, let each
Come back to the
Terra firma, and

Turn
Humanity
Into a magnifique
Candor's freedom…

Destiny

Let's look at
Our fate where
The world is
Changing too fast

Indeed, it's
Our survival as
A species is
In question today

Humanity's
Drowning into the
Senseless bigotry,
Violence's and wars
For a long

Only way
To win is
To strengthen
The inner Being
At the core

Let that essence
Awakening free us
From the tight jaws of
Seven sin, techno opiate
And the myopic mindset,
At once…

JAGDISH J. BHATT, PhD

Brings 45 years of academic experience including a post-doctorate research scientist at Stanford University, CA. His total career publications: scientific, educational and literary is nearly 100 including over 55 books.